day
notes
of
secrets

day
notes
of
secrets

jillian mukavetz

atmosphere press

table of contents

part I

part I

love is not a coincidence

similar lengths
like being mutually beautiful with someone.
I found her prayer
he found her rings.

citrus branch, a living here wish.

spines of a bow may have been obvious at one time.
their story like royal, in a first snow.

take it out on the clouds. obelisk and transient.
clean & paint
the left side of the sun.

silhouette

her   full body   strokes,
chalk, illustrates the
kitchen door.

conscious of her chest,   chest of spiral
of a wave

was she a boiled rose
a tsunami

she rose
fabric   frame, a rose

list

I will keep your something found,

a squashed gum wrapper.
mouse droppings in a candle cup.
stale fingernails, black with dirt.

winter waist tall weeds.
entangled car parts in a garden.
whimpering without a tongue.

the red whir of a snow cone machine.
unopened sippy cups.

relics & books.
silver tarnished and old oatmeal soap.
a single earring in the bathroom sink.

man cried and laughed so much today,
the hard part

about laughing is what comes,   after
get over the hair shit.
been laughing and crying
all day man
lost I was late

I paid him in full
he shook my hand.

learning music

comet
in the moonlight
a doe tongue, crunch
frozen
grey grass
take all of me.

more a fan of living my own porn honestly
in all color black through white

tranquil and shaded at this end of the track.

knowing that you are making love

the soft birthday kiss is on the curve
                between lobe ear & neck

my brain space
how stories   us and other
                               empathy exams

I love her even in capitals
honeyed fondness

or that loneliness. we always run to in the arms of stray,
away find comfort from and in within

nerves

where the seasons   collapse
a hand beaten
box of copper

a sacred collapse clay stone
mouthing the forgiving   brittle of a leather cord

she gives

my lineage shares the urn.
its blue crackled
crane lilac & blue
I wonder how she found it,
I wear her engagement ring on my left hand.

the highest peak

we lived in a warm, other worldly place with many lovely animals, cascading floors or rooms and softly chaotic happenings. we were mosaics, like attentive adventures just shared with, in life. when we went inside the coyotes started howling. like un flattened clouds, on canvas. we are already complete, driving on roads in un flattened clouds, on canvas.

just before

it's so quiet now, my little feels a bit like
an opal
a life   advent drawing

he couldn't stop talking how he hadn't been allowed to talk for years.

imagine her, a baby. salt
carvings,   many tens in sand
stilts in a

unhooked rib under the shoulder blade.

it does

I would consider cutting my hair, but it's so long
like octet is a heart
measures the perfect date.

it matters the killing of wisdom

let's go   *day*

in the early dark drift of pandan, the volcano breathes up cities, unsewn pocket buttons from everyone's hand lanterns. the fabric of bodies trying to capture the welcome clutch of the sun. sometimes. he told me. there is disappointment. as they, two hours later reach the top. and the sky is covered in clouds.

when she left, she had kind whale eyes. soft shell white skin. like the water skinned off all of their scales.

hex formed in fountains.

away this morning

we went to the beach with neighbors & there were many goats &
many sharks who enjoyed bouncing on the shore and doing ran-
soms like eating bushes before they scurried away. in this one mom
died, there was a demon next door who crawled into the house. we
ran away with your brother, found a missing cat who was a minia-
ture of the other. we climbed out of a black car, lost your wallet, had
no money in a mall with two cats. trying to find a box big enough
for two cats. no shoes two cats.

she passed this morning

my brother watched as I sprinted directing
the ambulance up the driveway

watched

you have to be a resident to park for free

rather than later

sonnet
addicted touch away my heart
sometimes neither
I thought, a humming bird
on the city   in my balcony

by the river

near the bank others bathe freely in the cool stream.
love, came by the river.

love & I were rock climbing amongst the
moss and little iridescent smooth pea pebbles.
love fell, breaking both feet.
they were smashed to little smooshy little red bits.
you had no feet.

in loves dream, I was attacked by a bear.
love had a large beige gash
across the cheek, and I several on my abdomen.
river took care of us, and we forgot about the interview.

if they say,

you were the first
disquote
tepid hypothesis

just before the temple, terrace. orange in three sounds

fond of I was he, as he was fond of me

let me loose
on the other side of a meadow   full of these plump, purple flowers

a picasso

the best lilac light
life beside an impressed lance,   is the ones they let in.

          even survivors saw the simple soldier best friends.
two pins were not enough

          barbaric like trees latch on to one another.
pears

red was sweet

they called me red was sweet.

lips me
a metal frayed silk   across my wrists
                           why does

there is some sweet madness, to any dance

in my dream I went
to a museum.

a strange place to go in a dream, or any
if you have fresh sheets.

I wish it was chilly and I had a bath

strawberry blond
          shadow contracts   in a beijing full moon

you found a pistol that was covered in bluish fingerprints. you wrapped it in newspaper & put it into your purple brocade purse. the body is wrapped in your ornamental carpet and placed in your car.

never higher I keep imagining falling. hes brother now. to the open planes, with the feathers again. I look closer. and see two cut jewels. he seems trying to hide something and assures me they are just nail shavings from some animal. with claws. clippings. I find him sitting on the sill in the bathroom as he dumps them out hastily to his right, into the sink, a clear vile with bits that make short ping sounds into the sink.

we carve the drop offs. I see straggly birds with fluffy down, blacks with bits of glitz. at the top is a woman with several boughfuls of elegant gold feathers.

balance

shy thing
when you
day notes, of pretend
sweet ones
sell
somethings
quite
hidden

temperance

to those in mention
she lushes
soft
pine giving up
justice. it
has it all on them.
like a fist, like the word *defeatist*
balletically firm
we tried to find a way and everything was done.

open doors

the note cools
the lake never had a sunset,
     the sunset never had the trees,
          the mirrors,
          were the same.

edible

a cardinal in pale carnation offers some rose sapphire jelly to my toast. a search for air now is a pink song. persimmons drench the wind. it is a hungry flower *rooted in the stem* you say in a silver say. a quick tongue. your reason candy tough, like wound sleep. the mist of your drips. here I am loving and insane, your breath.

inverse her life

its not often that one can say they were entangled with two
very living things
                              sound of an automatic
box frame bed
in an old thai serviced apartment

ribbon the first time autocorrect changes

live   to   *love*
he held my umbrella

part II

the pedestrian

he bends down to appreciate a given
moment yellow gratitude erased in even desire
just to be

center
perfect beach day sand shells the smell of gardenia perfume
the vibrancy
I was a new teacher & the house sitter was unkind

what he meant was
I haven't said in such a long time
I love you

the sole of the foot lowers into this undressed jungle. the color too ripe above the trace of neon. I am swallows inside of a thread wooded path. joints of orange jasmine the scent remains an un rip- ened clutch. we are the undercurrent of possibility. of this desire not to cradle the soft sandpaper pull of the skin. this temperature full weight. it is at once felt & imagined under the tongue sequined & sprouting. I part the green wig the parquet of flagstone. I need you to undo this zipped back. chiffon the prelude of plumeria too hot pink tucked behind the ear. fit a slip out of these notes this softness. I could be wearing nothing soaked wet like lotus leaves. your wrists in me wild with grace my swallows.

tame things

the reality on my rooftop draws him to want me.
the stars know why the moon is indigo again.
her glass box masturbates without a notice.
music just away is a glass box.
sometimes the reality wants you to fuck me.
innocence involved in the undeath of the streets.
dynamic paws wake up the coma.
a double sunlight in the flow of opal.
below the lovely beach draws me into her drawing.
two fingers balance the gentle staccato & chatter.
he carries the music up like a gondola.
the spring lights observe the overlook.
the flaws of a dove in the mouth.
the lightness offers space.
a learning of peach.

natures parchment

against the dayness, fresh & dewy
is pleasure the satin spar of stone.

I lick the un nouned boots
fold the hands, adjust crossed & envelope like
to rest on the dusted canary dress of the lap.

what is the diagonal of brandy
he finds her so quickly
trained things have no immensity

he kisses my lower lip dark

am I wrong

to love those
wooden fence eyes
porous something
to give what I have
seen missing
kiss heavy
dried paint turns into
sweat obstacle slick
the therapist hour a shank
he has already fallen
my sin, erase the
triangles and
suck me

balance the world

gentle touch of war stories on a freshly painted seat
see   breath like love notes

the maple the mahogany the iron
change must come first

a suitcase full of daisies.

I will play my violin today
it rises up
my electric wood three times the first.

a normal calm

the reality of flesh knocks on the window
good looking legs split the moon.

there is a music that wakes the sunlight
syncopated lunes heavy breath & thin nights.

a best friend you cannot keep your hands off of,
salty hands extend to the sea.

shadow putty in palms
what we crave we feed in sweets, to the blue jays.

wishes to burst

may be, just thunder
           utterly consumed rain
                   take this little box
                            let it go from me,
                            sandalwood,
                            the way you think of it
the validation was a snuggle, blush on the forehead,
a flicker this little acorn
when we first met time was a lost charm
molecules sway in rift. now underground in trees
           be careful to point to the moon, we could break it
           ocherish & glossy
           intent equals the breath equals
           the iris of the eye   the lattice   much more profound
    than its spikes.

is it easier when you call me

pornography and image soft the skin of the inner thigh

these nacred pearls
your body finds time
in the bright dorsal of the living
beside a wishing well   in the desert

at last the earth in light.

torn arrows

you cut my leash a heart of soft walls

touching you pleasure is to have a good time

limbs milky
beheaded
                hibiscus seeds in window boxes

touching you is a poem hung to dry like panties

in a trapped room
budding velvet inside of me
every petal

it is beautiful to intimacy

is it not,
                    what could have been.
a maneuvery of punctuation

the floor of things.
what my sex kinesiologist tells me my name means

how is one to do half way with all of this
never another soul

tonight I will desire

a person and their secrets.
lumbar & travertine   to wire it
to the light
to the bosom. awareness in

raining bullets, only the oversized steel rounds visible from the dawn
every day towards the simplicity of heart. as ephemeral, unlimited
draw or pull

tulip tree

rules
of doves

                              43

deeply listen. spring is unknown now
    grounded in a deeper   inside, inside of me

to hear her

I could taste the burned kite
lavender the stained
clouds.
                look, my tangled crown.
a whole rest, in the wake of long boats
a peaceful
sorbet sunday

I just wanted everything all at once.

an espresso,
a small pocket park, the size of a pocket park.

tincture

warmed tangerine
beyond thorn
a person to be your mirror
a meeting between the red husk of a gem,
simple as a
leather hunger   experiments & lime
thrust like balm,
in myriad   we slip through the river
repetition in stillness it ripples

light on self

only known by
I did not steal the book,
intention

simple, exhibits of
oxy toxin touch
with intention

a shared
only known by

of gratitude

accepting of partner play
violet white gypsy
walls line with murals
                                        swing
unconditional
                                              sway
there is some dormant
                          pulse
redress my love
and undress
                                              just as it is
stairs he draws for you

geraniums

above the shelf, the walls blink fractal blue light and watch as the children dip & dance along the everyday. they drop tips of copper coins into her black handbag dripping with ink. a resting under-growth appears, hand drawn. a reminder to draw in her shoulder rib and spin. the sacrum viewing the dense mist of dew. out of her jeans she pulls out a neatly quartered note.

remarkable

like the quiet warm exit red,   ruddy
trust against a rail, splits
  unfluted, hard blossoms in soft laces.

words inform the frame
chanting knives of sunflowers
a teak rope

woven walls of stickers slit a canvas.
a kidnapped galley.
the faint taste of nicotine on the tongue

sit me, with cinnamon in my chest beside the river. in the wall below the siamese carp, nip, at the water hyacinth. there's a chest behind me fabric wet. a stranger dream about me. a place where full gentle maps in the mouth, grow bulbous. butterfly tea with lime rests & a drop of burgundy. you break the core. come back, inside of me straddling the seal of the sun. daily groping is honey topaz in vinyl plum ceramic circles. shadows press the chamber. a blink in one eye. a milk shop door frame moves up, the spine like two delicate orchids, closing at night. a thunderstorm, close.

why remain the same

next to staccato, I into you, bliss
as safe, as I, with you
the moon would be damp
now a halo, a lamp
a soft path is stretched
time in hymns
we touch and give in
how could we say that you had never been
places where paradise begins

About the Author

Jillian mukavetz is a poet, photographer, musician, and founder and editor of *Womens Quarterly Conversation*. Her poems and photography have appeared in *Homestead Review*, *Verse*, *Coconut Poetry*, *Scapegoat Review*, *Delirious Hem*, *Ping Pong*, and *Ditch*, among other publications. Cinepoems have been published in *Harpy Hybrid Review* and *Otoliths*, as well as featured at film festivals in Big Sur, Denver, and Bangkok. Jillian plays the fiddle. Her chap books, *In the Process of Being Heard* and *Say Kitty, Kitty* are out from Dancing Girl Press.

Jillian has taught english in Bundang, South Korea; Bangkok, Thailand; Munich, Germany; and Beijing, China. Her masters include poetry and education. She is pursuing a degree in music production and currently lives and teaches in Lisbon, Portugal.